Color Your Day With Love

Chip the Monk

Harmony

Visionary and Author - Suzanne Sullivan
Co-Author and Editor - Pamela Breeze Bahr
Illustrator - Wendy Lorenzana

Copyright © by Chip the Monk Foundation 2023
All rights reserved.

ISBN: 978-1-7377493-6-3

Chip the Monk Foundation is a non-profit public charity operated exclusively for educational and charitable purposes within the meaning of Section 501(c)(3) of the Internal Revenue Code of 1986.
Tax deductible donations are gratefully accepted to support this important work.

Please visit our website to make a donation:
Chipthemonk.com

Facebook Page: Chipthemonk

Much gratitude goes to Rita Chance for her contribution to the inspiring content in this book.

Color Your Day With Love

with Chip the Monk and the Harmony Animals!

There is Dolly the Llama, who helps dissolve drama,
The Harmony Bees, who are always at ease,
Timidy the Turtle, who helps overcome hurdles,
and Holy the Cow, who lives in the WOW!

Can you find the Harmony Animals as you color your day with Love?

List three ways that you are kind to yourself.

Be kind to your mind.

And a little chipmunk will lead them...

Love is in the air!

It's so much fun to spend time together!

Chip Chip Hooray!

What scary thoughts do you want to shrink today?

Slow down your thinking and watch scary thoughts start shrinking.

Let worries go so your happy can flow.

Let all my thoughts be still.

If you are shy, then Timidy is your guy.

Even though he's small, he's a blessing to us all.

Holy the Cow helps you live in the WOW!

May your life be a love story.

May your day be filled with laughter.

Sing your favorite song!

One step at a time...

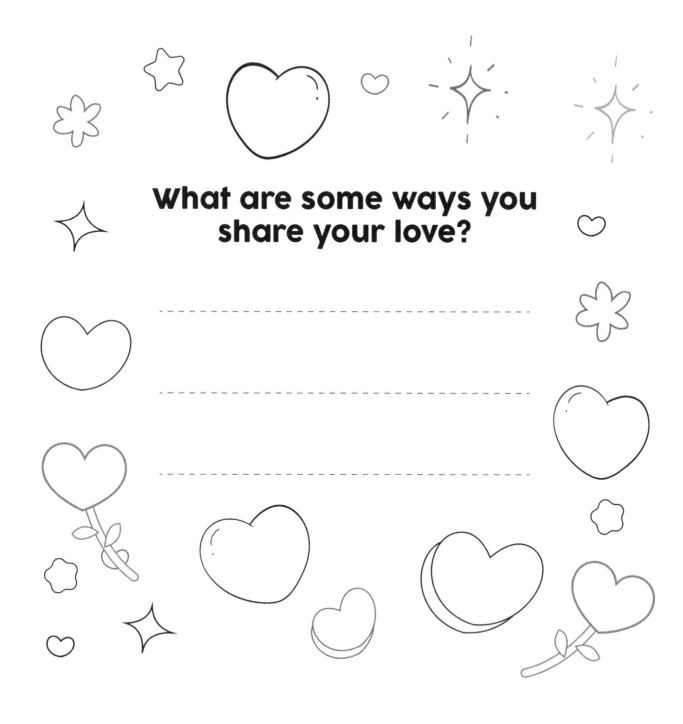

What are some ways you share your love?

Share your love.

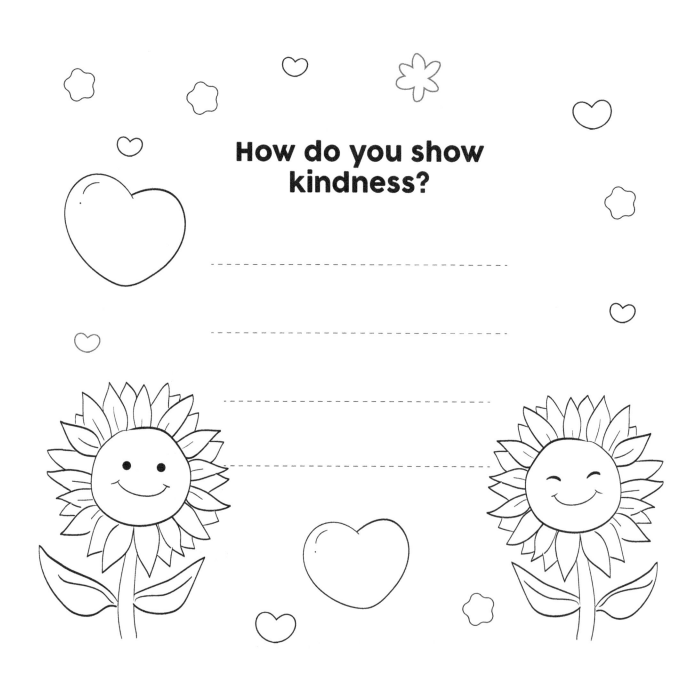

May your day be filled with kindness.

Color your day with care.

Flower power!

What are some of your favorite ways to play?

Remember to play.

Rest in Love...

Made in United States
North Haven, CT
18 July 2023